Contents

Christ ...

God Offers ...

Christ Resolves ...

God Grants Us ...

To:

_____

From:

_____

Date:

_____

199 Favorite Bible Verses for Graduates

© 2010 Christian Art Gifts, RSA
      Christian Art Gifts Inc., IL, USA

Designed by Christian Art Gifts

Images used under license from Shutterstock.com

Printed in China

ISBN 978-1-77036-438-7

18 19 20 21 22 23 24 25 26 27 – 24 23 22 21 20 19 18 17 16 15

199 *favorite*
Bible verses for
graduates

christian
art gifts®

God Knows Your ...

It's not your ability,

it's God's ability

flowing through you.

Benny Hinn

It is not my ability,

but my response

to God's ability,

that counts.

Corrie ten Boom

Abilities

1

God has given us different gifts for doing certain things well. So if God has given you the ability to prophesy, speak out with as much faith as God has given you.

Romans 12:6 NLT

2

Do not waste time arguing over godless ideas and old wives' tales. Instead, train yourselves to be godly. Physical training is good, but training for godliness is much better, promising benefits in this life and in the life to come.

1 Timothy 4:7-8 NLT

3

These are the gifts Christ gave to equip God's people to do His work.

Ephesians 4:11-12 NLT

4

"His master replied, 'Well done, good and faithful servant.' You have been faithful with a few things; I will put you in charge of many things.'"

Matthew 25:21

5

Do you have the gift of speaking? Then speak as though God Himself were speaking through you. Do you have the gift of helping others? Do it with all the strength and energy that God supplies. Then everything you do will bring glory to God through Jesus Christ.

1 Peter 4:11 NLT

6

So I run with purpose in every step. I am not just shadowboxing.

1 Corinthians 9:26 NLT

7

"To those who use well what they are given, even more will be given."

Matthew 25:29 NLT

8

Earnestly desire the higher gifts. And I will show you still a more excellent way.

1 Corinthians 12:31 ESV

I am only one,

but still I am one.

I cannot do everything,

but still I can do something;

I will not refuse to do

the something I can do.

Helen Keller

Ambitions

9

He who began a good work in you will carry it on to completion until the day of Christ Jesus.

Philippians 1:6

10

We are confident that He hears us whenever we ask for anything that pleases Him.

1 John 5:14 NLT

11

Make it your ambition to lead a quiet life, to mind your own business and to work with your hands, just as we told you, so that your daily life may win the respect of outsiders and so that you will not be dependent on anybody.

1 Thessalonians 4:11-12

12

One thing I do: forgetting what lies behind and straining forward to what lies ahead, I press on toward the goal for the prize of the upward call of God in Christ Jesus.

Philippians 3:13-14 ESV

13

Look to the LORD and His strength; seek His face always.

1 Chronicles 16:11

14

"Seek first His kingdom and His righteousness, and all these things will be given to you as well."

Matthew 6:33

15

I discipline my body like an athlete, training it to do what it should.

1 Corinthians 9:27 NLT

16

All glory to God, who is able, through His mighty power at work within us, to accomplish infinitely more than we might ask or think.

Ephesians 3:20 NLT

Character is the foundation stone

upon which one must build

to win respect. Just as no worthy

building can be erected on a weak

foundation, so no lasting

reputation worthy of respect

can be built on a weak character.

Anonymous

Character

17

The LORD bestows favor and honor; no good thing does He withhold from those whose walk is blameless.

Psalm 84:11

18

"Everyone who exalts himself will be humbled, and he who humbles himself will be exalted."

Luke 14:11

19

The Holy Spirit produces this kind of fruit in our lives: love, joy, peace, patience, kindness, goodness, faithfulness, gentleness, and self-control.

Galatians 5:22-23 NLT

20

"God blesses those whose hearts are pure, for they will see God."

Matthew 5:8 NLT

21

How can a young person stay pure? By obeying Your word.

Psalm 119:9 NLT

22

God is working in you, giving you the desire and the power to do what pleases Him.

Philippians 2:13 NLT

23

When your endurance is fully developed, you will be perfect and complete.

James 1:4 NLT

The purpose of

Christianity

is not to avoid difficulty,

but to produce

a character

adequate to meet it

when it comes.

James L. Christensen

Set yourself earnestly

to discover what you

are made to do, and then

give yourself passionately

to the doing of it.

Martin Luther King, Jr.

Purpose

24

"I have raised you up for this very purpose, that I might show you My power and that My name might be proclaimed in all the earth."

Exodus 9:16

25

We know that God causes everything to work together for the good of those who love God and are called according to His purpose for them.

Romans 8:28 NLT

26

He has showed you what is good. And what does the LORD require of you? To act justly and to love mercy and to walk humbly with your God.

Micah 6:8

The LORD will fulfill His purpose for me;
Your love, O LORD, endures forever.

Psalm 138:8

You can make many plans, but the
LORD's purpose will prevail.

Proverbs 19:21 NLT

Give thanks in all circumstances; for
this is the will of God in Christ Jesus
for you.

1 Thessalonians 5:18 ESV

30

I fully expect and hope that I will be
bold for Christ. And I trust that my life
will bring honor to Christ.

Philippians 1:20 NLT

The main thing in this world is not being sure what God's will is, but seeking it sincerely, and following what we do understand of it.

Paul Tournier

Until he extends his circle

of compassion to include

all living things, man will

not himself find peace.

Albert Schweitzer

God Is the
  Cornerstone of ...

The dew of compassion

is a tear.

Lord Byron

Compassion

31

The LORD is good to all, and His tender mercies are over all His works.

Psalm 145:9 NKJV

32

He tends His flock like a shepherd: He gathers the lambs in His arms and carries them close to His heart.

Isaiah 40:11

33

He heals the brokenhearted and binds up their wounds.

Psalm 147:3 ESV

34

You, O LORD, are a compassionate and gracious God, slow to anger, abounding in love and faithfulness.

Psalm 86:15

35

I still dare to hope when I remember this: The faithful love of the Lord never ends! His mercies never cease.

Lamentations 3:21-22 NLT

36

"You must be compassionate, just as your Father is compassionate."

Luke 6:36 NLT

37

The Lord waits to be gracious to you, and therefore He exalts Himself to show mercy to you. For the Lord is a God of justice; blessed are all those who wait for Him.

Isaiah 30:18 ESV

38

Praise be to the God and Father of our Lord Jesus Christ, the Father of compassion and the God of all comfort, who comforts us in all our troubles, so that we can comfort those in any trouble with the comfort we ourselves have received from God.

2 Corinthians 1:3-4

The best exercise
for strengthening the heart
is reaching down and lifting people up.

Ernest Blevins

If we all did the things

we are capable of doing,

we would literally

astound ourselves.

Thomas Edison

Confidence

39

As for you, be strong and do not give up, for your work will be rewarded.

2 Chronicles 15:7

40

The LORD will be your confidence, and will keep your foot from being caught.

Proverbs 3:26 NKJV

41

Be strong and courageous. The LORD your God will be with you wherever you go.

Joshua 1:9

42

This is the confidence that we have toward Him, that if we ask anything according to His will He hears us.

1 John 5:14 ESV

43

Be of good courage, and He shall strengthen your heart, all you who hope in the Lord.

Psalm 31:24 NKJV

44

I have set the Lord always before me. Because He is at my right hand, I will not be shaken.

Psalm 16:8

45

Blessed are those who trust in the Lord and have made the Lord their hope and confidence.

Jeremiah 17:7 NLT

46

The LORD is my shepherd, I shall not be in want. He makes me lie down in green pastures, He leads me beside quiet waters, He restores my soul.

Psalm 23:1-3

Optimism is the faith that leads to achievement. Nothing can be done without hope and confidence.

Helen Keller

Expect people to be better than they are; it helps them to become better. But don't be disappointed when they are not; it helps them to keep trying.

Merry Browne

Encouragement

47

"Do not be afraid! Don't be discouraged by this mighty army, for the battle is not yours, but God's."

2 Chronicles 20:15 NLT

48

May our Lord Jesus Christ Himself, and God our Father, who loved us and gave us eternal comfort and good hope through grace, comfort your hearts and establish them in every good work and word.

2 Thessalonians 2:16-17 ESV

49

The God of all grace, who called you to His eternal glory in Christ, after you have suffered a little while, will Himself restore you and make you strong, firm and steadfast.

1 Peter 5:10

50

The Lord your God fights for you, just as He has promised.

Joshua 23:10 NLT

51

Those who hope in the Lord will renew their strength. They will soar on wings like eagles; they will run and not grow weary, they will walk and not be faint.

Isaiah 40:31

52

The more we suffer for Christ, the more God will shower us with His comfort through Christ.

2 Corinthians 1:5 NLT

53

"I have told you these things, so that in Me you may have peace. In this world you will have trouble. But take heart! I have overcome the world."

John 16:33

Encouragement costs you nothing to give, but it is priceless to receive.

Anonymous

*Your life is short, your duties
many, your assistance great,
and your reward sure;
therefore faint not, hold on and
hold up, in ways of well-doing,
and heaven shall make
amends for all.*

Thomas Brooks

Perseverance

54

You need to persevere so that when you have done the will of God, you will receive what He has promised.

Hebrews 10:36

55

Let's not get tired of doing what is good. At just the right time we will reap a harvest of blessing if we don't give up.

Galatians 6:9 NLT

56

Consider it pure joy whenever you face trials of many kinds, because you know that the testing of your faith develops perseverance. Perseverance must finish its work so that you may be mature and complete, not lacking anything.

James 1:2-4

57

We rejoice in our sufferings, because we know that suffering produces perseverance; perseverance, character; and character, hope. And hope does not disappoint us.

Romans 5:3-5

58

God blesses those who patiently endure testing and temptation. Afterward they will receive the crown of life that God has promised to those who love Him.

James 1:12 NLT

59

Everything that was written in the past was written to teach us, so that through endurance and the encouragement of the Scriptures we might have hope.

Romans 15:4

60

Make every effort to add to your faith perseverance.

2 Peter 1:5-6

61

May the God who gives endurance and encouragement give you a spirit of unity among yourselves as you follow Christ Jesus.

Romans 15:5

In the confrontation between the stream and the rock, the stream always wins - not through strength but by perseverance.

H. Jackson Brown

The difference between

ordinary and extraordinary

is that little extra.

Jimmy Johnson

God's Word
  Teaches ...

Discernment is not a matter of simply telling the difference between right and wrong; rather it is telling the difference between right and almost right.

Charles H. Spurgeon

Discernment

62

"I will give you a wise and discerning heart, so that there will never have been anyone like you."

1 Kings 3:12

63

"The Helper, the Holy Spirit, whom the Father will send in My name, He will teach you all things, and bring to your remembrance all things that I said to you."

John 14:26 NKJV

64

The heart of the discerning acquires knowledge; the ears of the wise seek it out.

Proverbs 18:15

Reflect on what I am saying, for the Lord will give you insight into all this.

2 Timothy 2:7

Joyful is the person who finds wisdom, the one who gains understanding.

Proverbs 3:13 NLT

67

We are from God. Whoever knows God listens to us; whoever is not from God does not listen to us. By this we know the Spirit of truth and the spirit of error.

1 John 4:6 ESV

68

We have not received the spirit of the world but the Spirit who is from God, that we may understand what God has freely given us.

1 Corinthians 2:12

69

Preserve sound judgment and discernment, they will be life for you. Then you will go on your way in safety, and your foot will not stumble.

Proverbs 3:21-23

Integrity is not a given factor

in everyone's life. It is a result

of self-discipline, inner trust,

and a decision to be relentlessly

honest in all situations

in our lives.

John Maxwell

Integrity

70

Joyful are people of integrity, who follow the instructions of the LORD. Joyful are those who search for Him with all their hearts.

Psalm 119:1-2 NLT

71

The integrity of the upright will guide them.

Proverbs 11:3 NKJV

72

May God Himself, the God of peace, sanctify you through and through. May your whole spirit, soul and body be kept blameless at the coming of our Lord Jesus Christ. The One who calls you is faithful and He will do it.

1 Thessalonians 5:23-24

In my integrity You uphold me and set me in Your presence forever.

Psalm 41:12

May integrity and honesty protect me, for I put my hope in You.

Psalm 25:21 NLT

75

In everything set them an example by doing what is good. In your teaching show integrity, seriousness and soundness of speech that cannot be condemned, so that those who oppose you may be ashamed because they have nothing bad to say about us.

Titus 2:7-8

76

Light is shed upon the righteous and joy on the upright in heart.

Psalm 97:11

Integrity is the noblest possession.

Latin Proverb

God will not make you do something you don't want to do – He will just make you wish you had.

Wayman Mitchell

Priorities

77

"No one can serve two masters. Either he will hate the one and love the other, or he will be devoted to the one and despise the other. You cannot serve both God and Money."

Matthew 6:24

78

Look carefully then how you walk, not as unwise but as wise, making the best use of the time, because the days are evil. Therefore do not be foolish, but understand what the will of the Lord is.

Ephesians 5:15-17 ESV

79

"Where your treasure is, there your heart will be also."

Matthew 6:21

80

Good planning and hard work lead to prosperity.

Proverbs 21:5 NLT

81

"If anyone would come after Me, let him deny himself and take up his cross and follow Me. For whoever would save his life will lose it, but whoever loses his life for My sake will find it. For what will it profit a man if he gains the whole world and forfeits his life? Or what shall a man give in return for his soul?"

Matthew 16:24-26 ESV

82

Teach us to realize the brevity of life, that we may grow in wisdom.

Psalm 90:12 NLT

83

Whatever is true, whatever is noble, whatever is right, whatever is pure, whatever is lovely, whatever is admirable – if anything is excellent or praiseworthy – think about such things. Whatever you have learned or received or heard from me, or seen in me – put it into practice. And the God of peace will be with you.

Philippians 4:8-9

84

"Seek the Kingdom of God above all else, and He will give you everything you need."

Matthew 6:33 NLT

Thanksgiving is a good thing:

thanksliving is better.

Anonymous

Thankfulness

85

Since we are receiving a kingdom that is unshakable, let us be thankful and please God by worshiping Him with holy fear and awe.

Hebrews 12:28 NLT

86

May you be strengthened with joy, giving thanks to the Father, who has qualified you to share in the inheritance of the saints in light.

Colossians 1:11-12 ESV

87

Let your roots grow down into Him, and let your lives be built on Him. Then your faith will grow strong in the truth you were taught, and you will overflow with thankfulness.

Colossians 2:7 NLT

88

Thank God! He gives us victory over sin and death through our Lord Jesus Christ.

1 Corinthians 15:57 NLT

89

Thanks be to God, who always leads us in triumphal procession in Christ and through us spreads everywhere the fragrance of the knowledge of Him.

2 Corinthians 2:14

90

Give thanks to the LORD and proclaim His greatness. Let the whole world know what He has done.

1 Chronicles 16:8 NLT

91

Give thanks to the LORD, for He is good; His love endures forever.

1 Chronicles 16:34

92

Since everything God created is good, we should not reject any of it but receive it with thanks.

1 Timothy 4:4 NLT

Right is right,

even if everyone is against it;

and wrong is wrong,

even if everyone is for it.

William Penn

Values

93

Do not be conformed to this world, but be transformed by the renewal of your mind, that by testing you may discern what is the will of God, what is good and acceptable and perfect.

Romans 12:2 ESV

94

Who may worship in Your sanctuary, LORD? Who may enter Your presence on Your holy hill? Those who lead blameless lives and do what is right, speaking the truth from sincere hearts.

Psalm 15:1-2 NLT

95

If you are insulted for the name of Christ, you are blessed, because the Spirit of glory and of God rests upon you.

1 Peter 4:14 ESV

96

Imitate God in everything you do, because you are His dear children. Live a life filled with love, following the example of Christ.

Ephesians 5:1-2 NLT

97

The LORD is righteous; He loves righteous deeds; the upright shall behold His face.

Psalm 11:7 ESV

98

Let us behave decently. Clothe yourselves with the Lord Jesus Christ, and do not think about how to gratify the desires of the sinful nature.

Romans 13:13-14

99

Do not love this world nor the things it offers you, for when you love the world, you do not have the love of the Father in you. And this world is fading away, along with everything that people crave. But anyone who does what pleases God will live forever.

1 John 2:15, 17 NLT

In the midst of our triumphs

let us cry to God for humility.

Charles H. Spurgeon

Christ ...

Only those who respect

the personality of others

can be of real use to them.

Albert Schweitzer

Defines Respect

100

"Stand up in the presence of the elderly, and show respect for the aged."

Leviticus 19:32 NLT

101

Do nothing from rivalry or conceit, but in humility count others more significant than yourselves.

Philippians 2:3 ESV

102

Let love and faithfulness never leave you; bind them around your neck, write them on the tablet of your heart. Then you will win favor and a good name in the sight of God and man.

Proverbs 3:3-4

103

Respect those who work hard among you.

1 Thessalonians 5:12

104

"Do to others whatever you would like them to do to you."

Matthew 7:12 NLT

105

Show proper respect to everyone.

1 Peter 2:17

106

Love each other with genuine affection, and take delight in honoring each other.

Romans 12:10 NLT

107

Respect everyone, and love your Christian brothers and sisters.

1 Peter 2:17 NLT

Without respect,
love cannot go far or rise high;
it is an angel with but one wing.

Alexandre Dumas

Every time you make a choice

you are turning the central part

of you, the part that chooses,

into something a little different

than what it was before.

C. S. Lewis

Directs our Decisions

108

Solid food is for those who are mature, who through training have the skill to recognize the difference between right and wrong.

Hebrews 5:14 NLT

109

"I will lead the blind by ways they have not known, along unfamiliar paths I will guide them; I will turn the darkness into light before them and make the rough places smooth."

Isaiah 42:16

110

Your commands make me wiser than my enemies, for they are my constant guide.

Psalm 119:98 NLT

111

The LORD guides me along right paths.

Psalm 23:3 NLT

112

"In Your unfailing love You will lead the people You have redeemed. In Your strength You will guide them to Your holy dwelling."

Exodus 15:13

113

Seek God's will in all you do, and He will show you which path to take.

Proverbs 3:6 NLT

114

Show me the path, O LORD; point out the road for me to follow.

Psalm 25:4 NLT

We can do

anything we want

as long as we

stick to it

long enough.

Helen Keller

Laziness may appear attractive,

but work gives satisfaction.

Anne Frank

Favors Productivity

115

Now you are united with the One who was raised from the dead. As a result, we can produce a harvest of good deeds for God.

Romans 7:4 NLT

116

The LORD your God will bless you in all your harvest and in all the work of your hands, and your joy will be complete.

Deuteronomy 16:15

117

"Many who are the greatest now will be the least important then, and those who seem least important now will be the greatest then."

Mark 10:31 NLT

118

A tree is identified by its fruit. A good person produces good things from the treasury of a good heart.

Luke 6:44-45 NLT

119

"I am the vine; you are the branches. If a man remains in Me and I in him, he will bear much fruit; apart from Me you can do nothing."

John 15:5

120

Never be lazy, but work hard and serve the Lord enthusiastically.

Romans 12:11 NLT

121

Whatever you do, work at it with all your heart, as working for the Lord.

Colossians 3:23

The only place

where success

comes before work

is in the dictionary.

Anonymous

What makes humility so desirable is the marvelous thing it does to us; it creates in us a capacity for the closest possible intimacy with God.

Monica Baldwin

Models Humility

122

"Those who exalt themselves will be humbled, and those who humble themselves will be exalted."

Luke 14:11 NLT

123

"Blessed are the meek, for they will inherit the earth."

Matthew 5:5

124

He raises up the poor from the dust; He lifts the needy from the ash heap to make them sit with princes and inherit a seat of honor.

1 Samuel 2:8 ESV

125

The LORD sustains the humble.

Psalm 147:6

126

Humility and the fear of the Lord bring wealth and honor and life.

Proverbs 22:4

127

He leads the humble in doing right, teaching them His way.

Psalm 25:9 NLT

128

Therefore humble yourselves under the mighty hand of God, that He may exalt you in due time.

1 Peter 5:6 NKJV

129

The Lord takes delight in His people; He crowns the humble with salvation.

Psalm 149:4

Christian humility

is based on

the sight of self,

the vision of Christ,

and the realization

of God.

William Barclay

Aerodynamically the bumblebee

shouldn't be able to fly,

but the bumblebee doesn't know that,

so it goes on flying anyway.

Mary Kay Ash

Shapes Self-Esteem

130

Your body is the temple of the Holy Spirit, who lives in you and was given to you by God.

1 Corinthians 6:19-20 NLT

131

LORD, You have searched me and You know me. You know when I sit and when I rise; You perceive my thoughts from afar. You discern my going out and my lying down; You are familiar with all my ways.

Psalm 139:1-3

132

You made all the delicate, inner parts of my body and knit me together in my mother's womb.

Psalm 139:13 NLT

133

Not a single sparrow can fall to the ground without your Father knowing it. You are more valuable to God than a whole flock of sparrows.

Matthew 10:29, 31 NLT

134

How precious also are Your thoughts to me, O God! How great is the sum of them!

Psalm 139:17 NKJV

135

What are mere mortals that You should think about them, human beings that You should care for them? Yet You made them only a little lower than God and crowned them with glory and honor.

Psalm 8:4-5 NLT

136

You are God's own child. And since you are His child, God has made you His heir.

Galatians 4:7 NLT

137

"I knew you before I formed you in your mother's womb. Before you were born I set you apart."

Jeremiah 1:5 NLT

Honesty is the first chapter

in the book of wisdom.

Thomas Jefferson

Teaches Honesty

138

Who may ascend the hill of the LORD? Who may stand in His holy place? He who has clean hands and a pure heart, who does not lift up his soul to an idol or swear by what is false. He will receive blessing from the LORD and vindication from God his Savior.

Psalm 24:3-5

139

The LORD demands accurate scales and balances; He sets the standards.

Proverbs 16:11 NLT

140

Let your conversation be gracious and attractive.

Colossians 4:6 NLT

141

The plans of the godly are just.

Proverbs 12:5 NLT

142

"A tree is known by its fruit."

Matthew 12:33 NKJV

143

May integrity and honesty protect me, for I put my hope in You.

Psalm 25:21 NLT

144

God is good to those who are pure in heart.

Psalm 73:1

145

The Lord grants a treasure of common sense to the honest. He is a shield to those who walk with integrity.

Proverbs 2:7 NLT

An honest man
is the noblest work of God.

Alexander Pope

Examples are more forcible than precepts. People look at me six days in the week to see what I mean on the seventh.

Robert Cecil

God Offers ...

Is any pleasure on earth

as great as a circle of

Christian friends by a fire?

C. S. Lewis

Friendship

146

We know what real love is because Jesus gave up His life for us. So we also ought to give up our lives for our brothers and sisters.

1 John 3:16 NLT

147

"Greater love has no one than this, that someone lays down his life for his friends."

John 15:13 ESV

148

All of you should be of one mind. Sympathize with each other. Love each other. Be tenderhearted, and keep a humble attitude. That is what God has called you to do, and He will bless you for it.

1 Peter 3:8-9 NLT

149

A friend is always loyal, and a brother is born to help in time of need.

Proverbs 17:17 NLT

150

Perfume and incense bring joy to the heart, and the pleasantness of one's friend springs from his earnest counsel.

Proverbs 27:9

151

Share each other's burdens, and in this way obey the law of Christ.

Galatians 6:2 NLT

152

"I no longer call you slaves. Now you are My friends."

John 15:15 NLT

What is a friend?

A single soul

dwelling in two bodies.

Aristotle

Hang this question up in your houses – "What would Jesus do?" and then think of another – "How would Jesus do it?" For what Jesus would do, and how He would do it, may always stand as the best guide to us.

Charles H. Spurgeon

Guidance

153

"I will ask the Father, and He will give you another Advocate, who will never leave you. He is the Holy Spirit, who leads into all truth."

John 14:16-17 NLT

154

"I know the plans I have for you," declares the LORD, "plans to prosper you and not to harm you, plans to give you hope and a future."

Jeremiah 29:11

155

The LORD directs the steps of the godly. He delights in every detail of their lives. Though they stumble, they will never fall, for the LORD holds them by the hand.

Psalm 37:23-24 NLT

Your word is a lamp to my feet and a light for my path.

Psalm 119:105

We can make our plans, but the LORD determines our steps.

Proverbs 16:9 NLT

"Call to Me and I will answer you and tell you great and unsearchable things you do not know."

Jeremiah 33:3

159

Right behind you a voice will say, "This is the way you should go."

Isaiah 30:21 NLT

160

I will instruct you and teach you in the way you should go.

Psalm 32:8

Where God guides, He provides.

Anonymous

Conflict is inevitable,

but combat is optional.

Max Lucado

Christ Resolves ...

Use soft words

and hard arguments.

English Proverb

Conflict

161

A truly wise person uses few words; a person with understanding is even-tempered.

Proverbs 17:27 NLT

162

Whoever is slow to anger is better than the mighty, and he who rules his spirit than he who takes a city.

Proverbs 16:32 ESV

163

The wisdom that comes from heaven is first of all pure; then peace-loving, considerate, submissive, full of mercy and good fruit, impartial and sincere. Peacemakers who sow in peace raise a harvest of righteousness.

James 3:17-18

164

Gentle words are a tree of life; a deceitful tongue crushes the spirit.

Proverbs 15:4 NLT

165

Live in harmony with each other. Never pay back evil with more evil. Do all that you can to live in peace with everyone.

Romans 12:16-18 NLT

166

He who covers over an offense promotes love.

Proverbs 17:9

167

You must all be quick to listen, slow to speak, and slow to get angry.

James 1:19 NLT

168

A cheerful heart is good medicine, but a crushed spirit dries up the bones.

Proverbs 17:22

Christ alone can bring lasting peace –
peace with God – peace among men
and nations – and peace within our hearts.

Billy Graham

A bend in the road

is not the end of the road,

unless you fail

to make the turn.

Anonymous

Fear of Change

169

Lord, You remain the same forever!
Your throne continues from generation to generation.

Lamentations 5:19 NLT

170

Jesus Christ is the same yesterday,
today, and forever.

Hebrews 13:8 NKJV

171

Every good gift and every perfect
gift is from above, coming down from
the Father of lights with whom there
is no variation or shadow due to
change.

James 1:17 ESV

172

"I am the Lord, and I do not change."

Malachi 3:6 NLT

173

"Heaven and earth will disappear, but My words will never disappear."

Mark 13:31 NLT

174

The grass withers, the flower fades, but the word of our God will stand forever.

Isaiah 40:8 ESV

175

No eye has seen, no ear has heard, and no mind has imagined what God has prepared for those who love Him.

1 Corinthians 2:9 NLT

Don't fear change –

embrace it.

Anthony D'Angelo

A successful person is one

who can lay a firm foundation

with the bricks that others

throw at him or her.

David Brinkley

God Grants Us ...

Success is not the key to happiness. Happiness is the key to success. If you love what you are doing, you will be successful.

Albert Schweitzer

Success

176

Commit to the Lord whatever you do, and your plans will succeed.

Proverbs 16:3

177

Trust in the Lord with all your heart; do not depend on your own understanding. Seek His will in all you do and He will show you which path to take.

Proverbs 3:5-6 NLT

178

The Lord will make you the head, not the tail. If you pay attention to the commands of the Lord and carefully follow them, you will always be at the top, never at the bottom.

Deuteronomy 28:13

179

This Book of the Law shall not depart from your mouth, but you shall meditate on it day and night, so that you may be careful to do according to all that is written in it. For then you will make your way prosperous, and then you will have good success.

Joshua 1:8 ESV

180

We know that in all things God works for the good of those who love Him.

Romans 8:28

181

Commit everything you do to the LORD. Trust Him, and He will help you.

Psalm 37:5 NLT

182

My cup overflows with blessings.
Surely Your goodness and unfailing
love will pursue me all the days of my
life.

Psalm 23:5-6 NLT

183

May the LORD give you the desire of
your heart and make all your plans
succeed.

Psalm 20:4

When love and skill work together,
expect a masterpiece.

John Ruskin

If you want to feel rich,

just count all the things you

have that money can't buy.

Anonymous

Wealth

184

My God will meet all your needs according to His glorious riches in Christ Jesus.

Philippians 4:19

185

Not that we are sufficient of ourselves to think of anything as being from ourselves, but our sufficiency is from God.

2 Corinthians 3:5 NKJV

186

God will generously provide all you need. Then you will always have everything you need and plenty left over to share with others.

2 Corinthians 9:8 NLT

187

I have learned how to be content with whatever I have. I know how to live on almost nothing or with everything. I have learned the secret of living in every situation. For I can do everything through Christ, who gives me strength.

Philippians 4:11-13 NLT

188

Honor the LORD with your wealth, with the firstfruits of all your crops; then your barns will be filled to overflowing, and your vats will brim over with new wine.

Proverbs 3:9-10

189

Give freely and become more wealthy.

Proverbs 11:24 NLT

190

Teach those who are rich in this world not to be proud and not to trust in their money, which is so unreliable. Their trust should be in God, who richly gives us all we need for our enjoyment.

1 Timothy 6:17 NLT

191

God has given each of you a gift. Use them well to serve one another.

1 Peter 4:10 NLT

The more accurately

we search into the human mind,

the stronger traces we

everywhere find of the

wisdom of Him who made it.

Edmund Burke

Wisdom

192

If you need wisdom, ask our generous God, and He will give it to you.

James 1:5 NLT

193

The LORD gives wisdom, and from His mouth come knowledge and understanding.

Proverbs 2:6

194

Wisdom will enter your heart, and knowledge will fill you with joy. Wise choices will watch over you. Understanding will keep you safe. Wisdom will save you from evil people, from those whose words are twisted.

Proverbs 2:10-12 NLT

195

I will teach you wisdom's ways. When you walk, you won't be held back; when you run, you won't stumble.

Proverbs 4:11-12 NLT

196

Do not forsake wisdom, and she will protect you; love her, and she will watch over you.

Proverbs 4:6

197

If you call out for insight and cry aloud for understanding, and if you look for it as for silver and search for it as for hidden treasure, then you will understand the fear of the LORD and find the knowledge of God.

Proverbs 2:3-5

198

He will be the sure foundation for your times, a rich store of salvation and wisdom and knowledge; the fear of the LORD is the key to this treasure.

Isaiah 33:6

199

The fear of the LORD is the beginning of wisdom. All those who practice it have a good understanding.

Psalm 111:10 ESV

Notes

These extra pages have been provided for your personal reflections and thoughts ...

_____

_____

_____

_____

_____

_____

_____

_____

_____

_____

_____

_____

_____

_____

_____

_____

_____

_____

_____

_____

_____

Notes

Notes

Notes